spot

AWESOME NATURE

TREES

by K.C. Kelley

AMICUS | AMICUS INK

trunk

leaf

Look for these words and pictures as you read.

acorn

apple

What is that squirrel climbing?
It's a tree!

Trees grow around the world. Some trees grow in deserts. Others grow in water!

trunk

Look at this strong trunk.
Branches grow from the trunk.
Bark covers the trunk.

leaf

Look at these leaves.
Leaves soak in sunlight.
Some leaves look like needles.

apple

Look at these apples.
Many trees grow fruit.
Oranges, pears, and
lemons grow on trees.

acorn

See the acorns?

Acorns are seeds.

They grow into oak trees.

Trees are fun to play in.
We need trees!

trunk

leaf

Did you find?

acorn

apple

Spot is published by Amicus and Amicus Ink
P.O. Box 227, Mankato, MN 56002
www.amicuspublishing.us

Library of Congress Cataloging-in-Publication Data

Names: Kelley, K. C., author.
Title: Trees / by K.C. Kelley.
Description: Mankato, MN : Amicus, [2018] | Series: Spot. Awesome nature | "Spot is an imprint of Amicus."
Identifiers: LCCN 2017022568 (print) | LCCN 2017034352 (ebook) | ISBN 9781681513263 (pdf) | ISBN 9781681512860 (library binding : alk. paper) | ISBN 9781681522463 (pbk. : alk. paper)
Subjects: LCSH: Trees--Juvenile literature. | Readers (Primary) | Vocabulary.
Classification: LCC QK475.8 (ebook) | LCC QK475.8 .K45 2018 (print) | DDC 582.16--dc23
LC record available at https://lccn.loc.gov/2017022568

Megan Peterson, editor
Deb Miner, series designer
Patty Kelley, book designer
Producer/Photo Research:
Shoreline Publishing Group LLC

Photos:
Cover: Elena Elisseva/Dreamstime.com. Inside: Dreamstime.com: Alexander Potapov 1, Anthony James 2tl, Versh 2tr, Martin Novak 2bl, Viorel Dudau 2br, Yurasova 4, Rhbabiak13 6, Versh 8, Xalanx 10, Iakov Filimonov 12, Iurii Konoval 13, Feverpitched 14. Shutterstock: USBFCO 3, Lukas Gojda 9.